Marathon Diary

Written by Matilda May

Photography by Michael Curtain

Flying Start
to Literacy®

23 September

I saw my friend Annie at the park today. She is a Junior Marathon runner.

A marathon is a really long race – it is more than 42 kilometres. Annie said a marathon is exactly 42.195 kilometres.

I asked her how she runs 42 kilometres without getting tired. That is such a long way.

Annie said she doesn't run 42 kilometres in one race. She's been running nearly every day for eight weeks and she's already run 40 kilometres. She just needs to run the last 2.195 kilometres. Annie said that's what a Junior Marathon is – running one or two kilometres nearly every day for eight weeks.

Annie asked me to come and watch her at the finals. I think I'll go.

27 September

I went to watch Annie run the final part of the Junior Marathon today. There were lots of kids at the finals. They had log books to show that they had already run 40 kilometres.

Month September			ROUTE
Day	Distance	Time	
Monday 6	1.5	10:35	River path
Tuesday 7	—		Day off
Wednesday 8	1.5	10:15	Bridge run, back along Main street
Thursday 9	2	12:42	Two loops of the park
Friday 10	—		Day off
Saturday 11	2.5	15:21	Bridge run plus the river path
Sunday			Two loops of the park

When the run began, everyone cheered.
When Annie finished, she got a medal
and a certificate.

I want to try running the marathon too.

11 October

I got the information kit about the Junior Marathon today. It told me how to get ready for the run. It also gave me some great running tips.

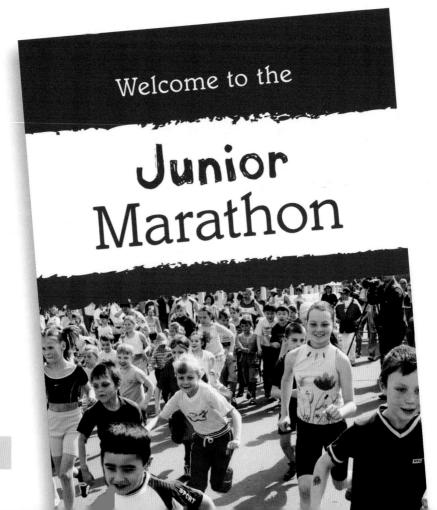

Welcome to the Junior Marathon

I also got a log book to fill in to show how far I ran each day. I don't know if I will be able to finish the Junior Marathon, but I am going to try.

Running tip

Keep a diary of your running. You can note where you ran, how far, what the weather was like and how you felt during and after the run.

12 October

Today I ran my first kilometre. I tried really hard. I was doing well until I reached the Porter Street hill. It is really long and steep and I got a stitch half way up and had to stop. Running was harder than I thought, but I'm not going to give up.

When I got home I asked Annie for some help. She said she would run with me sometimes to help me.

Only 39 kilometres to go!

Running tip

Start off slowly and don't try to run too fast or too far in the first few weeks.

14 October

Annie and I went running together today. She showed me how to stretch before running to help me run better.

When we started I ran quickly. I even ran faster than Annie.

Then Annie started yelling at me to slow down. She said you have to run slowly at the beginning so that you have some energy left to finish running the distance.

I slowed down but when we got to the Porter Street hill, I had run out of energy and Annie raced past me.

I was really puffing then, but I slowly made it to the top of the hill. Now I only have 37 kilometres to go.

Running tip

Running with other people can make running more fun and help you to keep up your fitness.

26 October

Today I read a book called *The Marathon Man*. It said that marathons first began in ancient Greece when a man ran from Marathon to Athens without stopping. That's amazing!

His city was in danger and he ran to get help. He was the first Marathon Man.

Chapter 4
The victory run

News had to be sent to Athens quickly. The people needed to be told that the enemy had been defeated at Marathon. And they had to be warned that the enemy ships were coming to Athens.

The soldiers looked at Phillip.

"I will do it," said Phillip. "I will run to Athens to warn the people."

Phillip ran for three hours over rocky mountains and he did not stop. He arrived at Athens in time to warn the people.

When the enemy ships finally arrived, the enemy soldiers saw that the people of Athens were prepared for battle. The enemy did not attack the city.

The Marathon Man

Greece

Marathon

Athens

5 November

Today Annie and I decided to run around the oval near my house. Annie said that it was good to run in different places.

The ground at the oval was flat so it was not so hard to keep running. I ran two kilometres without stopping. It felt really good. I've only got 24 kilometres to go.

Running tip
Look about three to five metres ahead and concentrate on running in a straight line. Keep your hands relaxed as you run.

16 November

I was feeling really fit today so I suggested to Annie that we run up the Porter Street hill.

We kept our breathing even and we ran as smoothly as we could. When we got to the Porter Street hill, I ran and ran. This time I didn't stop, even when I got a stitch.

Annie cheered me on.

Hooray! I made it to the top of the Porter Street hill – without stopping.

Only 14 kilometres to go.

Running tip

Try to get as much air into your body as possible by breathing deeply through your nose while you run.

4 December

Today I ran the 40th kilometre of my Junior Marathon – and just in time. The final is tomorrow. I can't wait.

I am feeling really fit and I'm sure that I can run 2.195 kilometres without too much trouble.

Annie and I are going to run together in the final.

Running tip

Wear shoes that are designed for running. The shoes have soft pads that help stop your body from being jarred.

7 December

Today was the final part of
the Junior Marathon. I was
really nervous before the race.
The other kids looked faster
and fitter than me.

I was worried I might have
to stop during the run, but
Annie said anyone who can
run up the Porter Street hill
can do this run.

I lined up with the others
at the starting line and
then we were off.

The first part of the run was easy.
I felt great. But as we ran further
I started to get tired. My legs
began to hurt. When they gave
me water to drink, I was so hot I
tipped it over myself to cool down.

I wanted to stop, but I kept running . . .

Running tip

Drink lots of water
before, during and
after you run.
Drinking water
replaces the water
your body loses
when you sweat.

. . . and I did it. I ran over the
finish line. I can't wait to run in
the Junior Marathon again next year.